The Protocols of the Goys for Sion

The wicked and secret plot by the gentiles

to defend Israel behind its back!

Pug

Goys defending Israel

SUMMARY

1 WHAT'S WRONG HERE

Little historical game that can be checked by anyone. Let's pick two majors characters of the israeli-arab conflict, born about the same time

-**Ariel Sharon**, by real name Ariel Scheinermann, born February 26, 1928 at Kfar Malal, in the British Mandate of Palestine and deceased at Ramat Gan, Israel, January 11, 2014.

-**Yasser Arafat**, by real name Mohamed Abdel Raouf Arafat al-Qudwa al-Husseini, August 24, 1929 in Cairo, Egypt and deceased at Clamart, France, November 11, 2004.

Ariel Sharon is the son of a Jewish couple from Eastern Europe that migrated to Palestine in the early 20's while nothing forced them to. They did it for love of the Promised Land and of hope for their children and became farmers there.

Yasser Arafat is the son of an arab couple from Palestine that moved to Egypt in the early 20's while nothing forced them to. His father was supposedly a shopkeeper from Gaza and the mother from

Jerusalem but it is not known for sure why they left Palestine.

Ariel Sharon spent his whole life in this land, first called British Mandate of Palestine and the Israel.

Yasser Arafat spent 4 years in Jerusalem during his youth and spent most of his life in Egypt, Jordan, Koweit, Lebanon, Tunisia and before moving to Ramallah, Samaria at the end of his life.

The young Ariel Sharon enlists in the Gadna, a jewish selfdefense militia and then in the secret jewish army, the Haganah. He fought in the 1948 Independence War and was severely wounded near Latrun during combat to liberate Jerusalem's Jewish Quarter's starving population from the Arab siege.

The young Yasser Arafat joins Jewish sports clubs in Cairo to know his enemy. He receives a commando training from a former Waffen SS officier. He is involved in supplying weapons to Palestine and spends the war as private secretary to his uncle, Haj Amin Al Husseini, Grand Mufti of Jerusalem, friend of Hitler and perpetrator of the Arab riots of the 20's and 30's against Jews.

Ariel Sharon becomes an officer in the Israel Defense Forces and works up the ranks with a sense of courage, example and tactical capability that makes him world famous and taught in military academies. His looks are those of the disciplined soldier of a regular army that defends its country. Even as a general, he will be wounded in combat several times. He is accused of war crimes while never being directly involved in the cases held against him. As a politician and Israel Prime Minister through democratic vote, he will go against the interest of his own people to lend a hand to the Palestinians

Yasser Arafat becomes a puppet of Egyptian leader Nasser who imposes him as head of the Palestinian movement, though he is in a ballot with a Syrian. His looks are chosen by Soviet advisors to create a symbolic figure like Che Guevara. Always safe and protected, he never participates in actual actions where he sends hundreds of fedayeen terrorists to confront the Israelis but also his Jordanian guests in 1970. As head of Fatah and Liberation Organisation Palestine, he is directly responsible for dozens of terrorist acts and crimes committed with his consent. Becoming the only leader of the Palestinian cause by eliminating his opponents and by political maneuvers, he will refrain from no lie, deception or betrayal to avoid making concessions to the Israelis. Incidentally, in 2003, he's the 6th World fortune in the Politicians ranking of Forbes magazine.

So let's see:

Ariel Sharon is seen as an invader of Palestine where he was born and Israel where he lived all his life and where he shed his blood to defend his people.

He's considered a barbaric and criminal war occupant.

Yasser Arafat is considered as fighter he has never been, and an activist of the liberation of a country where he wasn't born and where he has never lived.

He's considered a noble and respectable figure of resistance to oppression movement.

What's wrong, here?

2 A FEW THOUGHTS ABOUT PALESTINE

« "Well played, but it proves nothing and the reality of today, is a flouted Palestine and Palestinians suffering under the yoke of Israel who doesn't behave well at all in this case »

- The origin of the name "Palestine", said "Filastin" in Arabic, comes from the people of the Philistines, a people of Indo-European, and not Semite, traders, probably of Greek or Cretan origin, called "People of sea "by the Egyptians, and installed on the coast between Ashdod and Gaza, and who have always been the sworn enemies of the Israelites. And the Philistines take their biblical name from the Hebrew word "Peleshet" meaning "invaders" - Palestine, the Latin "Palaestina", derived from the ancient Greek "Palestina" is a name that appears in the 5th century BC in the writings of Herodotus, and later in those of Ptolemy and Pliny the Elder.

In these writings, the complete term used is "Palestine Syria" and never Palestine alone and "Palestine Syria" is described separately from Judea and Samaria. It was the Romans of the Emperor Hadrian in 135, which changed the name "Provincia Judea" and include it in the great province of "Syria Palaestina", following the Bar Kokhba Revolt , where two thirds of the Jewish population of Judea (the same rate as the Jews of Europe during the Holocaust), disappeared during the Roman repression.

The name of Palestine, to designate the entire region between Turkey, the Desert of Syria, Egypt and the Mediterranean, appears in the 11th century of our era, in the framework of a cultural cleansing of Hebrews in the region of Roman Empire. The name persists under the Byzantine Empire and then the Arabs and Turks Empires.

The Sykes-Picot Agreement between Britain and France in 1916, sharing this wide territory between the two great victors of the Great War. The Paulet-Newcombe Agreement of 1920, establishes the boundaries between the French Mandate of Lebanon and Syria and the British Mandate, called "British Mandate of Palestine" which includes the current territories of Israel and Jordan. The name Palestine disappears with the end of the British Mandate in 1948. From 1948 to 1967, the territory of the former British mandate is divided between three states: Israel, Egypt (Gaza Strip), Jordan (Judea and Samaria).

The name Palestine was brought back to the front scene in 1964, with the creation by Egypt of the Palestine Liberation Organization. Knowing that the Gaza Strip was then occupied by Egypt and Judea and Samaria by Jordan, the creation of the PLO clearly designated Israel as the territory to be liberated.

This name is claimed as the national appellation of a people pretending to fight against the "occupation", while at the same time, claiming a name meaning "invader" imposed by an occupant; One must dare!

These people - the Palestinians, hate Israel and they have good reasons to do so, according to the Pro-Palestinians brandishing publicly and mediatically unstoppable arguments to illustrate the cruelty of Israel toward the Palestinians.

Let us review some of these irrefutable arguments:

- *The Gaza Strip is one of the most densely populated areas in the world.*

The city of Gaza alone has a density of 9983 people per square kilometre. It is less densely populated than, in ascending order:... Delhi, Osaka, Geneva, Jakarta, Tokyo, Buenos Aires, Seoul, Paris, Mumbai, Shanghai, Cairo, Manila and Dhaka (Bangladesh). In the ranking of the most densely populated cities, Gaza comes just before Moscow and Grenoble. Just for comparison, Gaza has a density of 9983h / km2 and the most densely populated city in the world, Dhaka, has a density of 43 797 h / km2. This simple comparison is enough to undo the argument; the densite of the population in itself and alone, cannot be a cause of suffering of a people. Paris, Geneva and Tokyo, which are more densely populated than Gaza, are also the economic capitals of their respective countries and enjoy a higher standard of living than the rest of the country where the population density is lower.

- *The Gaza Strip is starving*

The Palestinians are in the top 10 ranking of global obesity, very close to the Americans. A Palestinian study indicates that in urban areas, 49% of women, 30% men and 16% of adolescents range above the threshold for obesity. Responsible are: the excessive consumption of soft drinks and hyper sweet desserts, and for women, the lack of sports facilities reserved exclusively for women according to the religious norms imposed by Hamas. One usually objects that obesity, does generally strike the most malnourished people, which here, is a false argument, since it is neither a question of malnutrition nor of junk food, but of access to foodstuffs which is absolutely not hampered.

- *The Gaza Strip is subjected to a blockade*

The only blockade of the Gaza Strip now under way is due to Egypt, which closed all the crossing points between Gaza and Sinai. On the Israeli side, many crossing points are open and are the entry points of all goods into Gaza, even during the fightings between Gaza and Israel. Moreover Israel supplies electricity, fuel and water to the Gaza Strip. Of commodities and energy entering Gaza, one cannot legally talk of a blockade, which is a total interruption and without exception, of the economic flows.

- *Palestinians experience a genocide* -

The average life expectancy of the Palestinians is 73 years and this is one of the best life expectancies in the Arab world. The Palestinian population grows spectacularly with a rate of 3.44% per year in 2013, a situation qualified as " Gaza demographic miracle ", thanks to a very high birth rate, a very low rate of infant mortality, and a long life expectancy. For comparison, the genocide of the European Jews saw the disappearance of 60% of the population and the genocide of the Assyrians (Aramaeans/Chaldeans/Syriacs) by the Ottomans, reached 75% of the population between 1915 and 1922.

- *The Palestinians are deprived of water by Israel*

A water deprivation generating a danger to humans under a Mediterranean latitude would immediately result in a sharp decline in the figures of life expectancy and by a drop in the demographic curve, which continues to rise. In addition, the opening of a Water Park in Gaza in 2010, immediately closed for religious reasons, by Hamas, seems antithetical to a shortage of water in the Gaza Strip. In terms of access to water, the Palestinians are far more victims of their own irresponsible behaviour on environmental matters and the significant resulting pollution.

- *The Palestinians have no access to education*

94% of Palestinians are literate; it is the second best rate of the Arab world after Qatar. The Assistance to Refugees Agency specially created for the Palestinians, the UNRWA financed by the UN, which manages many educational institutions and the international American and European aid among the most important, are also devoted to education. The Palestinian Authority claims that 80% of young Palestinians complete secondary studies. In the Gaza Strip alone, 8 higher education establishments, of university type, are available.

- ## *Palestinians defend themselves against the occupation by Israel*

The status of the "West Bank" and Gaza is not defined by any treaty establishing borders and sovereignty. The "1967 borders" never existed; there were only the 1948 armistice lines. The only recognized borders are those of Egypt and Jordan, which have returned to their original borders by abandoning Gaza for Egypt, and the "West Bank" for Jordan. These territories are legally disputed territories. Israel therefore does not occupy any sovereign foreign lands but does actually occupy a juridically empty space, and the legality of this occupation was attested by the Court of Appeal of Versailles in 2013 in the Jerusalem Tramway case. From an historical, geographical and legal perspective, Israeli claims on these lands are, at the very least, equally legitimate as that of the Palestinians.

Just have a look in historical archives or in Atlases of the start of the twentieth century, and you will find that the area south of Jerusalem, which includes the cities of Bethlehem and Hebron, has always been called Judea, a name that has the same source as "Judaism" and "Jew" and which derives from the name of the Kingdom of Judah, resulting from the secession of the Kingdom of

Israel, whose capital was Samaria whose ruins adjoin the Arab village of Sebastia, near Nablus, formerly called Shechem in the northern area of Jerusalem, whose geographical name has always been Samaria. This is the reason why, the "West Bank" has two authentic names, Judea and Samaria.

- *Palestinians are refugees who are entitled to return home*

For all other peoples of earth, the refugee status refers to those who have been displaced by force or exodus, and only those persons. Neither their children nor their descendants. If international law was equally applied between the Palestinians and the rest of the world, the only Palestinian refugees would be the people who were displaced between 1947 and 1948 and who are therefore, at 65 years old and over. The Palestinians born in Gaza, the West Bank, Jordan, Lebanon and Syria after 1948 cannot be regarded as refugees. Only one exception, therefore illegitimate, for the Palestinians, makes this situation unfair to all the other refugees on earth, starting with the 900,000 Jews expelled without compensation, from the Arab countries of which they were the inhabitants before 1948. Moreover, and contrary to the Jews expelled from Mususlman countries, the 1948 Arab refugees were not expelled by Israel, but have voluntarily fled the territories of the new state of Israel, not to be ruled by Jews and especially because Arabs leaders, who planned to reduce Israel to nothingness, called the Arabs to quit the territory of Israel so that their armies can safely finish the Holocaust and avoid burrs on Arab inhabitants. Besides, all the Arabs did not respond to this call, and those who remained and who were able, eventually, to benefit from a family reunion granted by Israel to their loved ones who fled, are the ancestors of the 1,6 million Israelis Arabs living, thriving and very happy in Israel.

- *Palestinians suffer from apartheid in Israel.*

"Apartheid" is a South African word meaning "Separated Development", designating the establishment from 1961 to 1994 of a separate development policy between white and black communities in South Africa. This word can neither be taken out from its South African context, nor from the historical context, of the history and mentality of the Dutch Protestants and the French Huguenots installed in South Africa in the XVII century, and constantly threatened by African tribes, as well as by British imperialism. The use of this word for the Israeli-Palestinian conflict demonstrates either an intellectual dishonesty or a profound ignorance of the history of South Africa and the Apartheid. In addition, Israeli citizenship is detained by 1.6 million Arabs, or the equivalent of the population of Gaza, and the Arab Israelis have access to all functions of the State of Israel or its parliamentary democracy. In fact, the State of Israel, practices an integration policy mixing Jewish populations, Arab, Druze and others, while the promoters of a two states peace solution, one Jewish and one Palestinian , actually advocate, a separate development solution of two communities, thus an "Apartheid" (let it be stated, once again, that this term can be applied solely to South Africa and its historical context)

3 APARTHEID

« Yes, okay, the South African Apartheid is a very peculiar concept but it does not change the facts that Israel practices what you mention as a separate development and favors the Jews on racist and nationalist criteria and this is what we resume by the word' apartheid '!»

Here are a few facts on which everyone will agree: That these unspeakable abuses against human rights must be stopped at all costs.

Everyone says it, especially in the great wisdom of objective and reasonable anti-Zionist demonstrations: Since the beginning of its modern history in 1948, Israel hates the Arabs and the Muslims and practices a terrible segregation towards them. It is time to denounce vigorously and without pretence this Israeli apartheid, and here are the irrefutable evidences:

-The racists and xenophobic Jewish Zionists fought against all Palestinian Arabs without exception in 1948, and since then, in a shameful discrimination, did not accept any Arab in their armed forces, as evidenced by the IDF Unity of Bedouins that paraded in Tel Aviv in 1949, and as evidenced today, the existence of the Druze Battalion Herev (Sword) and the Bedouin Battalion Desert Reconnaissance, not counting the number of Druses, Christians,

Arabs and Muslims who serve in the Borders-Guards Units or in the police, like the Druze policeman Zudan Sayef who sacrificed his life by intervening in the shooting of the synagogue Kehilat Bnei Torah on November 2014.

-The Israeli Jews feel so much disgust towards the Ethiopians and the Arabs that they have elected as "Miss Israel", Ms. Rana Raslan, an Arab Muslim in 1999 and Ms.Yityish Anyaw, an Ethiopian Jewess in 2013, who served as an officer in the Israeli Military Police, to emphasize their sexist side.

-The anti-Arab segregation in Israel is of such severity that it is an Arab Chretien, Judge George Karra, who condemned the former President of Israel, the Jew Moshe Katsav, to seven years in prison for rape, and a Christian Maronite Arab of Lebanese origin, Salim Joubran, of seats at the Israel Supreme Court since 2004.

-Israelis are such racists and sectarians, that in October 2013, they appointed Colonel Ghassan Alian, a Druse, as Commander of the Golani Brigade, one of the oldest and most prestigious units in the IDF. Numbers of IDF Generals are also Druze and receive commands as important as, for instance, the Interior Front.

-The Israeli society denies the Israeli Arabs so many legitimate democratic rights, that 14 Arabs sit as Deputes in the Knesset, and even have the right to rejoice in the kidnapping by Hamas of the three young Israelis boys in 2014, and even more, to be re-elected as the country's 3rd political force in April 2015.

-The Israeli Army is such a hangout of xenophobic Nazis that it has established several field hospitals which welcome and care for Syrian refugees fleeing civil war, and the Israeli Society is so inequitable that she treats the wife of Mahmoud Habas in her hospital , and the granddaughter of Ismail Haniyeh, the Gaza Hamas leader, the very man who calls for the death of Israel.

Good enough? Do you understand that this business of apartheid and discrimination against the Arabs has no basis, or shall I need to use further sarcasms?

The fact is that Israel is a multicultural country, multi-ethnic, crossed by many national influences that coexist all together, starting with the 1.6 million Arab Israelis, whose average standard of living is far more valuable than of the Arabs living in the neighbouring countries, and especially that of the Arabs living under the ferule of the Palestinian Authority and Hamas.

4 LAND AGAINST PEACE

« Okay but we must understand that the Palestinians have the right to self-determination and that everything could be settled if Israel gave land in exchange for peace!»

According to many observers and eminent analysts, the central problem of global geopolitics, the "mother of all battles" of international politics, is that only one Jewish state encroaches on Islam lands.

Let us recall certain facts:

Islam: 1.6 billion people in the world!

Judaism: 13 million people worldwide

Arab World: 300 million inhabitants

Israel: 7 million inhabitants

Number of Muslim countries at the UN: 56

Number of Jewish countries at the UN: 1

We must admit that the injustice done to Islam is unbearable

So obviously, the solution advocated by the US, EU, UN, etc, is self-evident: The Arab and Muslim countries not having enough with the Middle East, that they are emptying of all Christian influences after having emptied it of its Jewish influences in 1949, we have to ask Israel to make "territorial concessions " in exchange for peace!

Translation: Israel gives land to the Palestinian Authority and the Palestinian Authority in exchange gives peace to Israel.

This principle looks like great diplomatic wisdom for world peace, does it not?

Do we have examples of land exchange against Peace? Yes and quite a bitter example: In 1938, it was the promise made by Hitler to Czechoslovakia for the Pro-German Sudeten regions. Did it promote world's peace? Take stock of Europe in 1945, and you will have your answer.

Let's put it bluntly, and not in a civilized language: Land against peace is a war ultimatum, not a compromise for peace! It amounts to saying: Give me land, otherwise you have war, but saying it in a way that deceives only fools and politicians.

According to this principle, to avoid a war with Nazi Germany in 1939, Poland should have voluntarily agreed to cease to exist; to avoid war with Nazi Germany, the USSR would have voluntarily ceded its entire western part up to the Urals and keep only the steppes and Siberia. To avoid the war with Japan, China should have voluntarily agreed to be annexed by Hiro Hito. To avoid war with the Soviet Union, the free world would have voluntarily accepted the Communist International in the whole world, and to avoid war with the Fundamentalist Muslims, we should voluntarily accept the Islamic sovereignty and pay the infidels tax to the Muslims.

In France, to avoid the war, we should have, therefore voluntarily and even, spontaneously offered Aquitaine to the English, the Alsace-Lorraine to the Germans, the Languedoc to the Spanish, the Rhone-Alps to the Italians, without even talking about the minorities of the Basques, Bretons and Corsicans independentists, that we seriously offend with our refusal to spontaneously offer them their independence.

Moreover, Israel has already largely experienced this solution. In 1993, Israel signed the Oslo Accords giving 40% of Judea and Samaria to the administrative control of the Palestinian Authority, with the project to transfer the entire region to the latter by the year 2000. Also, in 2000 Israel has unilaterally withdrawn from Southern Lebanon which it retained as a buffer-zone against the actions of the Hezbollah. In 2005, Israel has unilaterally withdrawn from the Gaza Strip, by even expropriating thousands of Israeli "settlers" who lost all their efforts and their investments in this painful withdrawal.

The result was eloquent; The Palestinians triggered the Second Intifada in 2000 and started suicide bombings; Hezbollah presented as a military victory the Israeli withdrawal in 2000 and began harassment raids in Northern Israel which led to the 2006 war; The Hamas which preaches total destruction of the Jews, won the Palestinian elections in 2006 and fired nearly 12,000 rockets and shells, despite two major Israeli operations in 2008 and 2014 to try and stop them.

The only time Israel managed a land exchange for peace, was with Egypt in 1978 at the Camp David Accords. But the fact is that the issue of the land was not at all the fundamental point of the agreements and that Egypt manifested its will for peace before speaking of lands. Therefore, the retrocession of the Sinai to Egypt was a consequence of peace and not a misleading prerequisite.

In short, in the current state of the Israeli-Palestinian context, "land against peace" is only a disguise for a diplomatic war action that goes on since 1948 and still aims to destroy Israel as a Jewish Nation-State.

5 ARAB POLICY OF FRANCE

«Yes, it is cute and touching this idealistic defence of Israel , but you see, France has superior interests to defend, particularly where its strategic supplies and its trade balance are concerned, and this requires an Arab policy of France»

It is true, for the last 14 years, France is proud to have an Arab policy, beautifully symbolized by the Arab World Institute, founded by Valery Giscard D'Estaing with the assistance of twenty member-countries of the Arab League, and inaugurated by Francois Mitterand in the historic heart of Paris. Immune to political changes and installed in the 5th Arrondissement of Paris, not far from the centres of power, the Arab World Institute is the most perfect symbol of the French will to diplomacy and communication with the Arab world.

The most fervent defenders of the Arab policy of France trace it to the humanist clairvoyance of Francois 1er, who allied with the Ottomans in February 1536, thus giving France a privileged position in the Muslim world. It is confirmed by the expedition of Bonaparte to Egypt, by the long French history in North Africa as well as by the French proxy presence in Syria, which all testify to a deep attachment of France to a great Oriental and Islamic Culture, thus justifying the French diplomatic predispositions towards the Arab world.

But its real source is much more recent. The moment he came to power in 1958, President Charles de Gaulle attempts to restore France to an independent International stature. The re-conquest of this stature passes through three stages.

First, the acquisition of nuclear weapons and terrestrial vectors, submarine and aerial in order to implement it. In 1960 France becomes the fourth nuclear power in history and its Mirage IV aircrafts, like its intercontinental missiles of the Plateau d'Albion make their entrance on the strategic chessboard of the Cold War.

Second, the political and diplomatic independence in relation to the logic of the West-East blocks. While stating repeatedly its commitment to Western values, France separates itself from NATO, which must leave its territory in 1967.

Third, economic independence by securing energetic and strategic supplies. The significant development of the economy and industry during the Trente Glorieuses needs indeed to offset the loss of natural resources in Algeria by a policy of influence towards countries with strong natural reserves. In Black Africa, wherever the diplomatic context allows, France transforms its colonial rule in a political and economic game of influences derogatorily nicknamed "Francafrique". In the Muslim and Arab world, Algeria being out of reach due to violent liabilities, it was the advent of the Arab policy of France. By its influence and diplomacy, France intended to secure its energy and mineral supplies, necessary to its industry and its global strategic positioning.

We are not here to rewrite history with "if". In the Gaulienne vision of France, this strategy was theoretically absolutely right at the time it was decided upon. But after more than forty years, and in light of the events that occurred during this period, it is permissible, even essential, to try and establish an assessment of this policy, and take up the cost on several levels.

The first visible consequence of this policy was the decision by Charles de Gaulle of the embargo on arms sales to Israel. Indeed, since the early 1950s, France is the main supplier of weapons to Israel and often the only one. At a time when the market of armament is widely dominated by the USA and the USSR, which are hardly interested by the Arab-Israeli conflict, France is the only country to accept to sell weapons to the Hebrew State and she finds here a privileged market opportunity, particularly for its Marcel Dassault planes. The planes Hurricanes, Mystere IV, SMB2, Vulture, Noratlas but especially the famous Mirage III, will show their operational capabilities in the Israeli Heyl'A Avir which will benefit Dassault, of what is called today the feedback. The French AMX tanks will also have a significant market opportunity and operational test bed in Israel. Obviously, one of the most important areas of this Franco-Israeli cooperation concerns the nuclear industry.

This may seem insignificant but the 1967 embargo will have long-term repercussions on the French armament industry, even if it is still doing relatively well. It is not very healthy to address this question only from its commercial angle, but it is undeniable that before 1967, France is a leading supplier in the longest conflict after the war and where the requirements in armament and innovations are constant. With the French weapons, the Israelis won considerable victories, which are the best possible advertisement for French expertise and Israelis pilots will be the best of Dassault Sales Representatives - The Mirage III, valued and even adulated by Israeli pilots who will be the first Aces on a French aircraft since 1940. (In military aviation, the title "Ace" is attributed to any pilot who destroyed five enemy aircraft in flight. The Israeli General Giora Rom, pilot of Mirage III, will be the first Ace on the Mirage III at the age of 21 and Israeli Colonel Giora Epstein became the best Ace in history, on a jet, with 17 wins, all on Mirage III).

Depriving herself, as France did in 1967, of a major industrial outlet and an unrivalled trading showcase, is not without consequences in the long term. One can of course only assume what would have been the commercial operational career of the Rafale, which France is painfully trying to sell internationally for more than 20 years, if it had been operated during the 90s by the Israeli Air Force. It is perhaps significant that three of the biggest commercial successes in combat aircraft, the Dassault Mirage III, the McDonnell Douglas F-15 and the General Dynamics F-16, have all experienced or are experiencing a brilliant operational career in the Israeli fighters. The same analysis, more or less, can be made for the French tanks whose industry is disappearing, at very short notice.

It will be easily objected that many Arab countries have bought French weapons and thus largely compensated for this loss, which is probably true from of a simple financial point of view, but which is a very short-term vision. None of the Arab countries purchasers of French equipment have made such a good and spectacular use of it as Israel did and therefore did not contribute, far from it, to the reputation of French weapons, which were pitifully overmatched, especially during the Gulf War in 1991 .

Together with the arms embargo, the progressive remoteness of Israel will be the second consequence of the Arab policy of France. Even if it was not at all the prior intention, it is factual that France has gradually moved away from the only democracy, state of law with stable institutions in the Middle East, to get closer to autocratic states, despotic monarchies with feudal economies as the Saudi, and police dictatorships with planned economies of Marxist inspiration in the Mediterranean or in the Middle East. France makes the choice of economic and / or military relations renewed with Morocco, Tunisia, Lebanon, Syria, Iraq, Saudi Arabia and more recently Qatar. France sells arms to Morocco, Tunisia, Iraq and Saudi Arabia and develops strong diplomatic relations. We remember the proximity of Jacques Chirac with Sadam Hussein, for instance. The French choice of an Arab policy, initiated by De Gaulle and pursued by his successors is obviously linked to the oil supply, but it is also here that is found another unfortunate consequence of this policy.

ndeed, the French efforts towards the Arab world have never sheltered France from economic or political upheavals caused by regional tensions. In 1973, the crisis caused by the decision of the OPEC to increase the price of the oil barrel to unpublished proportions hit the French economy in the exact same way than other oil-importing countries. France will never receive any dividends for its Arab policy, whether on the economic or security level. In 1981, during the second oil crisis, France will not be spared either and continue diving into a deep crisis with high unemployment, which is still not settled more than thirty years later.

From a security standpoint, the French peacekeeping force in Lebanon will savagely be assaulted many times by the PLO, supported by many allies of France. The terrible ambush in which will fall in 1978 the future general Jean Salvan, injured 18 times and seriously disfigured, is the most striking example until 1983, where 58 French paratroopers died in the attack of the Drakkar post, attack fomented with the complicity of the Islamic Republic of Iran whose Supreme Guide, Ayatollah Khomeini, had nevertheless benefited from the protection and hospitality of France before overthrowing the Shah of Iran in 1979. The national territory, in 1985-86, will be the target of political Arab terrorist movements as the PLO or the Hezbollah which will cause 13 dead and 300 injured, the most serious being the attack in front of the TATI store on Rue de Rennes in September 1986. The years 1994-5 will even see France being among the first targets of Radical Islamism, with the diversion of the Algiers-Paris Air France flight in 1994 and the bombing of the Saint Michel station in Paris in 1995. The Arab policy of France has no more success in the relations with Colonel Gaddafi of Libya, who will sponsor the attack of the DC-10 "of UTA in 1989. Militarily, France was committed against Saddam Hussein's Iraq in 1991, against the

Taliban Fundamentalist Islam in Afghanistan between 2002 and 2013, against Muammar Gaddafi's Libya, and against Al Qaeda Islamic Maghreb, heir of his old 1995 enemies, the Islamic Algerian Armed Group in 2012, and against the Islamic State in 2015. And one could fairly easily relate to this sad list, the Karachi's attack in 2002.

Terrible symbols, in 2012, the killings in Montauban and Toulouse by Mohammed Merah, a French citizen, repeated in 2014 by Mehdi Nemmouche, a French citizen, and in 2015 by the brothers Kouachi and Amedi Coulibaly, French citizens, as well as the attacks- attempts by Sid Ahmed Glam, a French citizen and Ayoub El Khazzani, a Moroccan attempting an attack in France, all Radical Muslims, put an end, if need be, to any angelic belief on the relations between France and the Arab-Muslim world.

If it was, maybe theoretically, justified in 1967, with regard to France international situation, France Arab policy can only be considered, More than forty years later, as a terrible and shameful fiasco where France attitude, compared to its ideals of state of law and democracy are made perfectly illegible and made of incessant bends according to events. The French ambiguity on Iraq, friend of Saddam Hussein in 1978, ignoring the war crimes and crimes against humanity (Halabja, 1988), enemy in 1991, de facto neutral between 1991 and 2003, to becoming near- allies to the UN Security Council through the voice of Dominique de Villepin, is more than enough to summarize this fiasco, but we must not keep silent as to the hospitality to the Ayatollah Khomeini, the lack of reaction when

Hezbollah kept Lebanon under a dangerous double sovereignty, the volte-face within a few months, in front of Muammar Gaddafi and Bashar El Assad, the proposal of assistance made by the French Police to Ben Ali against the riots of the Arab Spring, the indolence shown to the Hamas's bloody takeover of the Gaza Strip and the falsely naive recognition of Palestine to the UN claimed by the heirs of the PLO in November 2012, confirmed by the resolution of the French Parliament, the National Assembly and the Senate, on the "Palestinian state" in November and December 2014.

The French position is totally illegible and indicates an incomprehensible procrastination between economic success' imperatives and strategic supplies and the republican ideals of free democracy, enlightened and responsible. Worse, this unreadable position causes a new anti-Semitism that hides behind anti-Zionism and a hostile attitude toward Israel, the only stable nation in the Middle East which shares the democratic state of law model, supposed to be based on the values of the French Republic. By playing the game, by strategic calculation, of the Arab sensitivity by always condemning Israel and crying over the Palestinians, that we finance blindly, while maintaining diplomatic and economic relations with Israel, France lets one think about Israel, that hidden forces "hold" her. Thenceforth, the idea of a financial American-Zionist plot, prevents France to take up completely the Palestine cause, comes naturally to weak or devious minds, already influenced by the ambient anti-Zionism of the French Left and the open or latent anti-Semitism of Islam.

How to recognize oneself in this totally materialistic policy that goes against the values of Republican France, and goes on endangering those who are like us? How to make the French citizens adhere to a republic which practices an official form of corruption and betrays its own values on behalf of its own interests? How to inspire respect for the nation and the republic to France's youth, especially the one of foreign origin who must integrate the history and values of France, if we, we betray them?

France did not manage to obtain the security of its strategic supplies or its economic security. But she attracted the hatred of many people and the incomprehension of many of her own citizens who have the dreadful feeling of a generalized corruption and have less confidence in their leadership and their institutions.

More than ever, facing an Arab world that continues to detonate with delay like a gigantic sub munitions-bomb, partly due to the procrastinations and ambiguities of the great democratic nations supposed to stand fast onto their values to which she belongs, France must regain her founding values and the principles of the Enlightenment Century, that made her switch her values. She must stick to them at all costs, and renew the sacred covenant with the free nations that share them and firmly oppose any compromise or materialistic deviations or interest, even if this means paying the oil quite a lot more. Much better, and by far, a country in economic difficulty, but firm and stable in its values and its world view, than these diplomatic and political sugar coats that never protected us from anything, but undermined our values, undermined our principles, and have sown confusion, both among our true friends, as well as among our own citizens, especially the younger ones.

It is time to courageously end this "Merchants of The Temple" diplomacy which sells off our values for financial gain and an electoral advantage in the INSEE statistics, and as long as we will not have common society values with those countries, and moreover, at a time when research and innovation allow us to hope getting rid of alliances which are against nature, we must put an end to the very idea of an Arab Policy of France, an abject whiff of a colonialist paternalism and the hidden consequence of a failed decolonization.

Yes, it is a question of courage, of idealism, even yet of a little ingenuity. It is about personifying the values of freedom, of equality, of fraternity and of asserting, by a coherent diplomacy, stable and firm, that faith in our values and our principles cannot be initiated by economic issues and to impose a clear position that France cannot be reduced to its strategic and commercial needs.

6 THE ISRAELI MODEL FOR FRANCE

« Yes, it is fine to criticize, and this Republican Enlightenment idealism is touching by its naive silliness, opposed to our high level of intelligence and diplomatic realpolitik experience, but other than that, concretely, what do you suggest? »

As it happens, comparing the recent history of France and the Jewish people holds some surprising similarities that may suggest that the example of Israel is an example to meditate upon, for our old country is so frightened by modernism and change, that it thinks having to choose between slavery and the installation of an iron curtain.

You may rather judge :

One of the worst periods in the history of the Jewish people, the Holocaust coincides with one of the worst periods in the history of France, the Occupation. The coincidence however is not one. The French inaction, facing Hitler in 1935 when he broke the Treaty of Versailles, through the creation of the Luftwaffe in 1936, with the remilitarization of the Rhineland and the Anschluss of Austria, and in 1938 during the Sudeten crisis, gives him a free hand for his mass murder program. The more France kept quiet, the more the concentration camps and the power of the Wehrmacht, grew. The French collapse leading to the occupation is the "blank check" that

Hitler needed for his extermination program. Nothing would have been possible had France stood up to him while he was still weak, and nothing would have been possible if France would have fought effectively. Hitler knew it, and he feared you. But we collapsed in the worst shame of our history and Hitler had a free hand in Europe to implement the final solution to the Jewish question. When France no longer had the right to sing the Marseillaise, the Jews were sent to Auschwitz.

The French reconstruction after the national tragedy of the occupation also happens close to the time of the Israeli construction after the tragedy of the Holocaust. In 1946 France adopts the constitution of the IV Republic. The Jewish people are given a land to make a state, at the UN vote of November 1947 on the partition plan of Palestine. While French democracy is reinstalled, Israeli democracy is founded in May 1948.

In 1956, Israel and France fight together against a common enemy, supported by a common enemy. Socialist Nationalist Gamal Abdel Nasser's Egypt nationalizes the Suez Canal with the Marxist blessings of the USSR. At the time France is nearly the only country which agrees to sell arms to Israel. Those are French planes that equip the Israeli Air Force, and the Israeli paratroopers jump from French planes, dressed in French camouflage!   One must stress that the first Israel war after its independence was conducted alongside France, with French uniforms and equipment and the Israeli successes either in aviation or on board tanks, will be the best advertisements for our industry armament.

And while France fight the National Liberation Front also supported by the USSR, in Algeria, Israel sees the Liberation of Palestine Organisation created with the advice of the Soviet propaganda, slowing growing. It might be a coincidence, or not, but the PLO was formed in May 1964 on a model of nationalist socialism of liberation, against colonialism, which just got proven against France, 18 months earlier, in September 1962, with the Independence of Algeria, at the Evian agreements.

There is no need to recall the phenomenal successes of the Israeli Army during The Six Days War in June 1967 and the role, acclaimed by the best Israelis pilots, of the French Mirage III, which demonstrated during this conflict, that the French weapons were widely at the level, even outclassed the Soviet armament that stood up to the Americans, then in Vietnam.

The 20 years after the war when France and Israel are friends and Allies, are the 20 best years for the development of France. Despite the military failures and political instability, the French economy is reborn, develops and provides, thanks obviously to American aids, splendid economic successes, social and commercial. This is the period called "The Glorious Thirty" when the future smiled at France, proud of its past and looking to the future.

Unfortunately it is in 1967 that everything starts rotting. Anxious to balance the French strategic position, General de Gaulle pulls France out of NATO and decrees an embargo on arms destined for Israel. This is to break with the confrontation of the NATO blocks - {Warsaw Act) and secure France's supply of hydrocarbons from the Arab oil countries. The following year, France plunges with dismay into some slightly Marxist student revolts in May 1968, and in April 1969, General de Gaulle quits the Presidency of the Republic after his failure at referendum.

Five years later, on October 1973, Israel lives its darkest period with the Kippur War, that puts the Israeli army through a rough ordeal and instils doubt in Israel as to their survival. During this conflict the OPEC triggers the first oil shock destined to all those who support Israel. But despite the 1967 embargo, France does not escape the economic repercussions that affect the world. While the crisis begins in France, a crisis which, to date, never frankly ended, the commercial market outlets of our arms industry start drying up. The Mirage III sold very well, as per the AMX-30 tank. We will sell some Mirage F1 and a few Mirage 2000, to some Arab countries impressed by the prowess of the French aircraft. But 40 years later, the Leclerc Char and the Rafale, no longer find customers and will probably be the last products 100% French of our arms industry.

Since 1967, France conducted a foreign policy that is pragmatic, securing its supplies at the expense of its values. One does note calculate the numerous compromises of France with Arabs or African dictators who enter through the front door in the Humanity Museum of the horrors.

From Chemical Iraq to Genocidal Rwanda, through Zaire, Ivory Coast and Pakistan, the slates left by the French diplomacy are beginning to weigh very heavily on the national consciousness of a country that feels, rightly so, losing its values and identity in favour of foreign influences, either by immigration of people who do not want the French identity but only its redistributive model, or by the attraction exercised by foreign cultures with firm and proud identities.

Faced with this national consciousness at half mast, those who led us to this dead-end by their disastrous policies never stop designing enemies and pernicious influences they intend to fight to ensure the sustainability of the French model, even if musty. Higgledy-piggledy , the European Union , the Euro, the US, the liberalism, WTO, NATO, or the financial markets, are regularly accused by our modern Fouquier-Tinville who are never very far from accusing the Jewish banker, Israel, Zionism, the Axis Tel Aviv-Washington, the Israeli apartheid, etc .. Some moreover, downright and greedily pour into it, "liberalism" and "Jewish banker", NPA, being intrinsically associated in the French mentality which, incidentally, is regularly the dunce cap in Europe and worldwide, for the teaching and the knowledge of fundamentals and economic principles in its educational system.

For all these public prosecutors who send to the guillotine of their vindictiveness all those who, they believe, are suspected of betraying the ideals not really French but frankly Marxist, France is the Last edge of the Guard of some redistributive and statist social model, surrounded and threatened by Wellington's Anglo-Saxon liberalism and the Blucher of German Christian Democracy, financed and supported by the Israeli Rockfeller. And they will be happy to tell them the Mot de Cambronne and die stupidly taking with them the whole of France rather than surrender to the evidence of their blindness and their stupidity.

In the current torment of France, it might be beneficial to regain the friendship and alliance of Israel. Rest assured, this is no conspiracy theories where rich Americano-Zionist bankers will illico save   France! This is a simple and elementary homecoming and where France is finally true to her values, even at the cost of a higher Gulf oil price, and diplomatic tensions with Arab theocracies, with African dictatorships or the Chinese market. France must reassert its unchallenged commitment to parliamentary democracy state of law model, based on free responsible citizens, making individual conscious   choices   for   the   common   good. France must stop playing the diplomatic and propagandist games imposed by political terrorists such as the Palestinian Authority, Vladimir Putin or the Chinese Communist Party. France must reassert her values, recover the principles that led to her failed revolution of 1789-1792 and must make courageous choices. A powerful symbol of this French return to what she should indeed be, would be the recognition of Jerusalem as the sole and indivisible Capital of Israel and the right of return for the Jews to the whole of the land they were dispossessed of, 2000 years ago, especially in the ancient heart of the Jewish nation, Judea and Samaria.

But even more, it would help France to observe Israel with curiosity and a desire to learn, because Israel is like us: an old country, in a young state, which holds fast to its linguistic and cultural particularity, to its independence, to its integrity and its identity. Yet while we French who are at peace, have a panic terror of the future, of modernity and foreign influence, Israel is a nation at war, that has an immense faith in the future, which is at the forefront of modernity and which is crossed on all sides by foreign influences in this most variegated "melting pot" in history.

Israel is a nation more than 3000 years old. France is a nation more than 1000 years old. Israel has drafted its constitution in 1948. France has drafted its own in 1958. Israel is a country of 8 million inhabitants on a land as big as a French region. France is a country of 66 million inhabitants on a land as big as an American state.

They are in full development, with total confidence, have full employment, flood the world with their innovations, revolution medicine and agriculture and proudly brandish their culture, their language, their faith and identity that nothing and no one ever managed to make them disappear. They even succeed in encroaching onto the sacrosanct American showbiz by developing TV programs bought at the price of gold by American producers.

We are in full decline, in total distrust of each other; we never fell below the 8% of unemployment these last 40 years. Our health system runs out of steam, our agriculture, although the second in the world, lives only on grants and culture, language and French identity continue to doze, not even mentioning a faith that desert churches and temples to let young disturbed offenders fill makeshift mosques, harangued by mad preachers. As for showbiz, we have artists subsidized for their mediocrity by a Ministry of Culture and we have TV programs that lead us straight to the drugstore to buy antidepressants (reimbursed by a Social Security running out of steam). Highlight of the show, movies and French artists who make it in the world are here, despised with a snobbish and elitist arrogance.

How do the Israelis manage to be so open to all cultures and penetrated by so many different influences and yet be one of the proudest and most independent cultures there are? How do the Israelis manage to be so optimistic about the future when they are surrounded by so many threats and so much horror, sometimes even in their homes?

How do the Israelis do to develop such an economy in a land with so few natural resources, surrounded by so many countries without economic market outlets and which continues to welcome new immigrants?

How do Israelis do to remain faithful to their ancient and ancestral identity while being among the spearheads of progress, innovation and modernity?

France has here an example from which she must inspire herself on many levels. These are not Scandinavian social democracies. These are not the liberal Anglo-Saxon models. These are not the Chinese or North Korean protectionism. The model she should study is a small country which like her, is an old proud nation that wants to keep her identity and wants to transport it, intact into the future.

7 PRO-ISRAELI?

« First you claim that we should not reduce France to its business and here, you explain that your only appeal to Israel, is what she could bring us in terms of a development model! So, all that for a simple matter of materialism?»

No, far from it. All that for a simple question of the authenticity of the values, of communion of thought, of common roots and also of an unavoidable dose of historical legitimacy.

The Jews are nowadays probably the oldest non-primitive people in history. While all other ancient peoples were cleaned off in conquests and other assimilations, the Jews trace their history in a direct line to the first ages of Antiquity, almost at the gates of Prehistory. From the beginning of their existence, first as the twelve brothers, founders of the twelve tribes of Israel, they were fiercely independent and free. Yet they were slaves in Egypt, you will retort! Yes, but their liberation was the subject of the first great anti-slavery struggle of history, which almost brought the powerful Egypt to its knees. Biblical myths, not historical, you will say! Maybe, but even if one considers this narrative as a myth, it remains a founding myth of the Jewish nation, which therein characterizes its commitment to freedom and independence.

Becoming a Nation-State, they never were a great empire and never felt the need to be. It is perhaps one of the rare people in history who have always been satisfied with its piece of land. Once the initial conquest of Canaan passed, the land promised by God, they never pursued an imperialist desire on their neighbours, in spite of incessant wars with them. The only people, who have been completely conquered and destroyed by Israel, were the Amalekites, which represented such a threat to the survival of Israel that God ordered its full destruction. In his order, it was clear that it was not an economic conquest of war, but a war of survival, as no loot, no enrichment was to be drawn from this tragedy. The Amalekites had to be destroyed and completely, including their possessions and livestock. The disobedience of King Saul to that order will cause his fall under divine wrath. Religious nonsense, you say again? At least, and you cannot sweep it as easily, a legend kept in the constituent myths of the Jewish people mentality, since recorded in the Torah.

They had, all the same to conquer and slaughter the peoples of Canaan to settle there, it is often said, and yet it is untrue. Strangers wishing to live among the Jewish people were fully accepted.

Israel is one of the first nations to codify a status for strangers and of the welcome to a stranger while among her people, which is inscribed in the Torah, and the history of Israel is also constituted of foreign characters, fully integrated and even instrumental in the destiny of Israel. Ruth the Moabite is not Jewish and yet becomes the ancestress of King David, who himself entrusts important missions to strangers such as Hushai the Archite, sent to spy on his son Absalom rebellion, or even poor Uriah the Hittite, who, before being trapped by David who covets his wife, is one of the officers of the royal army. Moreover, this crime will earn the King a dramatic response in what he holds most dear and that will make him understand, that he is not above the law, at a time when the arbitrary absolutism is the norm in other nations and kingdoms.

Besides, the narratives of the Kings and Chronicles of Israel show a very particular and very precocious form of separation of powers. The Law, promulgated by God, applies to all, including the King himself, who cannot avoid it without being reminded by the Prophets of God, acting as a judiciary, and not hesitating to thwart royal decisions or impose measures to the government of Israel, or of Judah after the secession. This lack of royal absolutism is evident in the episode or Queen Jezebel, a Sidonian princess, accustomed to have everyone serve her at her beck and call, who cannot understand that her husband, King Ahab is powerless when the ordinary citizen Naboth refuses to sell him a field.

At the crossroads of great empires, the two Jewish kingdoms of Israel and Judah will always resist the major powers, always tempting, by all means, to preserve their independence or to restore it, once lost, in antique illustration of the peoples' right to dispose of themselves.

This perpetual will to freedom will bring them, incessant wars against their neighbours' imperialism many times in history; it will be only through blood, ashes, deportations and the complete destruction of their cities and capitals that Jews will be submitted. Even the term of submission is here hackneyed, as generally, there nothing left to submit, the materiel destruction but also socioeconomic being so complete. The Babylonians and the Assyrians Kings will have to besiege Jerusalem and take multiple times, deport first the Jewish elites and install puppet governments that too, will rebel to restore the independence. Nebuchadnezzar II will destroy Jerusalem completely and deport most of the Jewish people to Mesopotamia, the reason why important Jewish communities still existed in Iraq and Iran till the middle of the twentieth century. The Romans will go even further by destroying Jerusalem in 70 AD almost stone by stone, massively deporting the descendants of those who returned from Mesopotamia, to create a new government if not independent, at least autonomous. They will go to the extent of renaming it Aelia Capitolina, to signify to the Jews that they were definitely torn off their land, their traditions and their heritage.

Yet despite everything, while the Egyptians, Assyrian, Babylonian, Persian, Greek, Roman, Muslim and Ottoman Empires disappeared, the Jewish people still lives, always attached to its land, its traditions, its language, its heritage. This spirit of resistance to imperialism and totalitarianism, yet overpowering facing the Jewish weakness, made them cross the centuries and bury all their enemies, adding to this list the European kingdoms that segregated or even expelled them,

Tsarist Russia who invented the word Pogrom, the 3rd French Republic who yelled "Jewish traitor" during the Dreyfus Affair, the 3rd Reich which decreed their extermination and the USSR that discreetly continued the Tsarist persecutions. For almost 19 centuries, while integrating as best they could, to survive in their different adopted countries (one could nearly say "countries of concentration", in the Nazi sense for some), they never stopped repeating at every Passover: "Next Year in Jerusalem", indomitable and fierce in their desire to return home and regain their nation. Which people can say as much? The Assyrians disappeared and Babylon is an open museum. The Persians have disappeared and Suze with them. The Romans even them, abandoned Rome to Ravenna. The Byzantines mixed with the Turks and forgot Constantinople. The Gauls no longer exist and no one even knows anymore where Alesia actually is.

Their astonishing capacity of resistance to adversity is even confirmed by the four wars in forty years since the establishment of the State of Israel in 1947. No army, no equipment, no trained soldiers and without supplies, crushed by an arms embargo and a glaring numerical inferiority, they reversed the trend and saved their fledgling new nation, in feats of arms for which the word "glorious" is almost week. In 1956, in 1967, in 1973, irrespective of their opponents and their number, they have dominated, resisting even beyond reason. It is often said that in war, it is the most motivated that prevails and the Jews have demonstrated every time an exceptional motivation and courage to move mountains.

One can hate them because they are stateless, because they kept their culture, their traditions, and their faith. One can despise them because they have not become nearly like- us . One may want to exterminate them because one thinks they are parasites forming a sub-race. Or on the contrary, one can detest them because of this resilient independence, fierce and gentle at the same time, that "chosen people" arrogance they have learned not to express. Whatever form of hate they generate, they have crossed the centuries with their history, their traditions, their language, their faith, with tenacity and courage. What astonishing paradox, that Hitler, who swore only by a people pure and rooted in history, a superior race capable to resist, survive and triumph of all its opponents, picked on precisely the only people that perfectly suited this definition !

The previous chapter has evoked it, and without going into details of numbers and graphics, it is a fact on which all historians and economists agree. Only two countries have managed the feat of becoming a developed country, from scratch, over a period of only fifty years and those two countries are South Korea and Israel. Upon returning to their ancestral land without natural resources comparable to petroleum, and starting from an underdeveloped region of the Ottoman Empire, the major activities of which were, pastoralism, handicrafts and fishing, Israel is today a country at the peak of the high-tech industry, information technology, medicine, and high level surgery, industrialized agriculture, in particular by reversing the phenomenon of desertification to increase its arable land, unique in history. The standard of living is quite comparable to Western nations, with similar life expectancy. The education system is excellent and Israeli universities produce every year engineers, scientists and intellectuals of international level. We must of course consider that this development is done despite the constant threat of neighbouring countries that recognize only very gradually the existence of Israel and some major regional powers still refusing to do so. The country is surrounded by radical Muslim terrorist groups, Hezbollah in Lebanon in the north, the Martyrs of Al-Aqsa Brigade and the Islamic Jihad in the West Bank to the east, Hamas in the Gaza Strip in the west, and salafistes groups tied to Al Qaeda in the Sinai in the south.

Despite the conventional threat from neighbouring countries and the ongoing terrorist threat, the economy and the Israeli society are doing very well. Israel is a free, democratic, based on the state of law, guaranteeing freedom of expression and freedom of the press. To be convinced just consider the incarceration of a former president convicted of sexual assault and rape, the virulence of heads of the army's interviews by the Israeli press in 2006, during the Operation Cast Lead in Lebanon. The political alternation works very well, the three major parties of the left, centre and right succeeding one another or even completing each other in coalition governments that do not paralyze the institutions. The electoral process is tried and is conducted smoothly with a level of integrity entirely comparable to Western nations.

From the point of view of citizenship, Israel is a model country in terms of integration. Though Jewishness and the Jewish immigration are essential factors of integration, they are not exclusive. The acquisition of Israeli citizenship is very open, as evidenced by Christians and Muslims Israelis of different ethnic origin. The integration of Jews from around the world is also a marvel of openness of society, each community contributing its difference to the large Israeli community. The variety of languages, origins and cultures within the Israeli society make it one of the largest and most successful "melting pot' in the world and in history.

A remarkable thing to be emphasized, as a sign of the vitality of the Israeli society, the rehabilitation and the resurrection, as a living and official language, Hebrew, which had reached the status of dead language and for a long time remained confined to religious Jewish rites. Another stupefying sign of the ability of resistance of these people and their indomitable attachment to their identity.

It is easily seen that the historical and traditional principles of the Israeli society, above mentioned, continue to irrigate the modern Israeli life and institutions: the equality before the law, the denial of any tyranny, the separation of powers, the reception and integration of strangers. The more one reflects and analyzes the Jewish functioning, the more one realizes that our Western political model of freedom and individual responsibility of the citizens in a democratic state of law, open and tolerant is very clearly influenced by the traditional Israelite model, and not only by the ancient Greek model or Christianity, regularly invoked.

The existence of modern Israel and the natural application of these principles in its midst, in spite of the centuries of exile and various political influences is also a particular evidence of the universality and lasting quality of these values when we do not forget them or we do not choose to give them up or twist them, and this is one of the most obvious arguments, for who wants to understand them, that supporting Israel is essential to one that believes and wants to defend them.

8 BUT WHAT ABOUT THE PALESTINIANS?

« Ok, but there is a big problem in all your reasoning! The Palestinians. We cannot pretend they do not exist!"»

No, indeed, but we must define them calmly and out of any political argument. Back to History.

This has been evoked, the word "Palestine" was established by the Roman occupant, after they destroyed what was then called Judea, destroyed Jerusalem, have its people scattered, and even, during a period, banned them from entering this land. Roman cruelty was proportional to the attachment of the Jews to their land. To destroy all forms of Jewish resistance to the Roman rule, the method was to proceed to a true moral rape, tempting to durably denature up to the earth. By "Romanising", by Latinizing the names or reinventing them, by promoting the settlement of desert nomads and scattering the Jews in small persecuted communities in the roman world, the Romans hoped to uproot definitely the dream of independence and Jewish sovereignty over their land.

Despite everything, history shows that Jews have always tried to come back. During the conquests by the Arabs and then by the Crusaders, the Jewish population is a minority but quite real. During the Muslim period, Jerusalem and ancient Judaea, henceforth called

Palestine, are only one area of the various Muslim empires. Moreover, an area without any great appeal and without any economic and/or major cultural development. Apart from the sacred character of Jerusalem for the Muslims, although the Qur'anic text seeming to design Jerusalem is subject to interpretation, this land represents for Islam only a conquest and a part of the Ummah, the community of believers.

On the other hand, also undeniable, the idea of an Arab nationality comes to light only under Ottoman rule and the nationality is not so much linked to the earth as to ethnicity. When the British conquered Palestine in 1917, there is no Palestinian demand. But there is an Arab nationalist frustration, and encouraged by the British to rebel against the Ottomans, the Arabs dream of a great Arab state covering from the Mediterranean to the Euphrates and from the desert of Yemen to Syria.

And in this nationalist movement that will see the creation, for the Kingdom of Hejaz the flag they name today Palestinian, the Arabs wishes are not of a Palestinian state, but the integration of Palestine into a great Arab state which would be an Arab revenge on the Ottoman Caliphate.

In a general manner, the Palestinians' attachment to this land, has nothing in common with that of the Jews. The only time in history that Jews had a country, a state, laws, governments, was on this land, they did not want any other, and did not want more of it. Their only political and spiritual capital has always been Jerusalem. For Arabs and Turks, it was only an underdeveloped region of a great Muslim empire continually expanding, whose capital was either in Baghdad, or in Damascus or in Constantinople, the spiritual centre of which, was at the Mecca and Medina before being in Jerusalem.

When the Jews of Eastern Europe began emigrating to the Ottoman Palestine in the late 19th. century, under the influence of Zionism, it is already quite some time that, despite everything, the Jews are the majority in Jerusalem and live in Palestine, which everyone, including the Ottoman civil authorities as well as the Muslim religious authorities, regard as the historic land of the people of Israel as exposed by the Koran itself.

Moreover, this emigration of men, know-how and capital makes Palestine once again attractive for Arabs and is desired by the Ottomans. Selling land to Jews brought unexpected funds that irrigate the local economy, which knows a steady growth, with an impact on employment. Palestinians see their living standards rise, their living environment become civilized. Many can get out of pastoralism to become farm workers, craftsmen or traders.

But, if the Jews have in their religious and traditional codes, an integrated status for strangers, Muslims are religiously not allowed to live under any sovereignty other than Muslim and when the Zionist claims to autonomy and the independence take too much importance, tensions and conflicts break out and fester until the Partition Plan in 1947. This plan is accepted without negotiation by Israel that is assigned a coastal strip and a desert, leaving the nicest part to the Palestinians who reject it in the name of "all or nothing" and choose the ordeal of strength to try and regain in blood, lands legally sold and an economic fabric they never knew how to create and reject any idea of sharing, negotiation and conciliation with the Jews, not hesitating to claim they would throw them back into the sea.

The Palestinian tragedy lays in this perpetual denial of sharing and negotiation. After their defeat of 1949, rather than accept the verdict of weapons and establish a peace that could have led to a negotiated solution acceptable to all, Arab leaders called their populations into exile, throwing hundreds of thousands of compatriots in refugee camps in Lebanon and Jordan, to leave Palestine entirely free for actions of war and re-conquest facing Israel. But they never conquered it back and they let the situation of the refugees rot and become a security problem for Jordan, which will solve the issue by a blood bath in September 1970, and for Lebanon which, unable to cope with a "State within a State", that Yasser Arafat's "PLO represented, sinks into a civil war that will last 15 long years. Since, whatever peace plans, roadmaps, negotiations and other attempts at conciliation, the Palestinians perpetually choose the strong way, the confrontation and conflict, imposing on Israel an impossible choice and laying conditions they know are untenable for the Israelis leaders. This perpetual conflict, of which they are in turn, the voluntary hostages, can be solved, according to them, only by Israel's misfortune.

So what about the Palestinians? Alas, it is not so much about the Palestinians as of the Palestinian cause. In a land the Arabs have never been able to develop, have not been able to exploit, have not managed to valorise, the Palestinian claim can only be a farce.

Who would create a state to return to misery, to under-population and underdevelopment, which was evident before the Jewish emigration from Europe in the 1880s? What do the promoters of the Palestinian cause propose? Since the 20's and the first actions of Hajj Amin al-Husseini, the historical leader and evil soul of the Palestinian cause, it has been only about capturing power, corruption, incompetence, fraudulent enrichment, riots, exactions, murder and crimes against humanity. At best, they propose a vague adaptation of an economic planning inspired by the pan-Arab socialism which does not cease to collapse wherever it has been implemented, leading to the rise of radical Islam and the villainous violence, ethnic and religious, a cocktail already much in vogue among Palestinians. The Palestinian cause, seconded to the dream of a great Arab and Muslim state from the Euphrates to the Mediterranean and from Yemen to Turkey no longer holds any form of legitimacy or credibility. Who has further interest in the Palestinian cause? Only a Palestinian elite hungry for power and wealth, based on Arab-Muslim nationalism, inspired by Nazi theses and supported by an Arab world more or less nostalgic of his greatness, is still interested.

The Palestinian individual in all of this has no value. His life, his development, the future of his family, all this does not matter. What matters is that he serves, through its real suffering or his staged one, to justify the Palestinian cause and legitimize a Palestinian state that will never be legitimate. From the cradle, he is familiarized with weapons, with battle outfits, with explosive belts. From childhood, he is taught to hate the Jew, held responsible for all the suffering of the Islamic nation.

From adolescence, he is hardened to throw stones against IDF tanks, he is trained to stabbing Jews, he is taught the handling of rockets or the secrets of a well-oiled propaganda. If he reaches adulthood, he will have children he, in turn will indoctrinate without second thoughts, in the tradition of anti-Jewish hatred which he inherited.

Why ? By ancestral and religious hatred of the Jew that must be submitted to the precedence of Islam, and slaughter if he resists, and for dreams of Islamic Unity of the lands conquered in the 7th and 8th century. The legitimacy of the Palestinian cause is in this terrible project that has not aged since 1948: Throw the Jews into the sea and get rid of Israel.

Jew-hatred is the only reason for all this infamous genetic manipulation of human history. To continue to attack and harass Jews, a people were created from scratch, whose only reason for living is to justify the hatred of the Jew and, ultimately, fight and exterminate him. Suffice to see where the Palestinian cause has grown from to be convinced. The historic leader of the Palestinian cause, Haj Amin El-Husseini spent the Second World War in Berlin, had encouraged the formation of Muslim SS units, was personally involved in the final solution to the Jewish question by handling with Eichmann the deportation of Bulgarian Jewish children who died in Nazis camps, and by being perfectly informed by Himmler in person, of the goals and methods of the Holocaust. After the war, former SS officers will supervise the Palestinian Fedayeen, while criminals against humanity were recruited by Syria or Egypt as advisors against Israel. Even today, the enemies of Israel, Hezbollah, PLO, Fatah and Hamas, use Hitler salute, refuse to teach the Holocaust and glorify the Fuhrer. This Palestinian cause, which is none other than the continuation of the Nazi anti-Semitism by other means, has artificially created an entire people. Is it surprising when its instigators thought they could eliminate an entire people the same easy way?

The Palestinian cause, alas, is only a gigantic crime against humanity: The breeding and totalitarian slavery of millions of people for the sole purpose of hatred and extermination of the Jews, for purposes of power by a caste of corrupt oligarchs getting rich and playing at the table of the greats of this world, relying on a "Frankenstein" people, created solely to eliminate another.

This is an unspeakable horror and an unsustainable perversion.

And the only way out, the only hope for development and peace for this people oppressed and exploited by its leaders is undoubtedly, supreme irony, the state they have been taught to hate more than they love the life: Israel

Simply because Israel is the only country in the Middle East where Muslims or Christians fear nothing and where the Arab citizens of Israel are happy, prosperous and have the chance of a future.

9 OBJECTION!

« No, no, no, no and no! We have been told for 40 years: Israel is the imperialist, capitalist colonialism and any defence of Israel falls within an apology of fascism, of the oppression of minorities, the denial of democracy and is contrary to all humanist values»

Yet, defending Israel is anti-colonialist: it is defending the rights of Jews to occupy and manage their ancestral land without having to submit to the advice or to the oppression of a Arab Muslim or Turkish or European Christian colonial authority.

Yet, defending Israel is anti-imperialist: It is defending the right of Jews to resist against the Arab-Muslim imperialism surrounding them and seeking to destroy their ethnic particularism, cultural, national and religious to impose its supremacy on the Southern - Mediterranean before tackling the entire Mediterranean basin.

Yet, defending Israel is anti-capitalist; It is defending the Israelis workers, farmers, engineers, inventors who made from a desert wasteland, without any natural resources, a developed democratic country with advanced agriculture high-tech industries against the outrageous financial power of the autocratic and racist ruling caste of oil producing countries, that exploit the poverty stricken Pakistani, Indian, Arab and even Palestinian workers, engage in an uninhibited global corruption towards worldwide politicians and destabilize the economy and geopolitics at the discretion their whims, to then buy, with a vengeance, assets in countries they later sabotage.

Yet, defending Israel is antifascist: It is defending the Jews against the Nazi heritage that inspired the theses of the Palestinian cause and against the violence against them in Europe and the USA in the name of a Neo-Nazi and Extreme-Right anti-Semitism, and we defend Israel against the threat of Arab socialist nationalism crowned with a militarism inspired the fascism of the 30s, of Israel's neighbouring countries.

Yet, defending Israel is to take the defence of minorities: It is defending the 8 million Israelis against the 300 million Arabs who want the destruction of Israel, supported by several million of anti-Zionists, and we defend the 13 million Jews in the world against the, more or less 1.6 billion Muslims wanting their extermination or who would turn a blind eye to such a crime, supported by multimillion Western nationalists and Catholics Fundamentalists who want revenge for a deicide and the remaining millions of Westerners who would not give a damn if that happened.

Yet, defending Israel is to take the defence of democracy and humanism: It is defending the only parliamentary democracy and state of law based on freedom of the citizens, which works for more than 60 years amid a conglomerate of policed autocracies, and feudal religious monarchies which completely despise the elementary rights of the human nature and persecute their populations to remain in power, if necessary, by great blows of crimes against humanity.

10 DEFEND TO THE VERY END

« Yeah, but we're not Jewish or Israeli so who cares, it's not our war. It is suspicious when one is not Jewish to defend Israel and those who do certainly have hidden reasons!»

Which ones?

"They are Mossad agents!"

And they also killed Kennedy, kidnapped Marilyn Monroe who still has not aged, dynamited the Twin Towers and enjoying the Saucisson Festival every weekend with Osama Bin Laden.

"The Jewish bankers hold them by the giggleberries!"

Today, frankly, it is rather the French state with its stifling government and its highest taxes in the western world that holds everyone by their giggleberries...

"They are fans of Patrick Bruel!" (French Jewish Singer and Actor)

Patriiiiiiiiiiiiiiiiiiiiiiiick !!! Although more as an actor than a singer but no, sorry. Nay if we hate him, it's because our girlfriends were in love with him when we were teenagers and they still are after twenty years because he aged well, that scumbag...

"They are bloody white racists who hate the Arabs"

Racist and "Friend of the Jews" in the same sentence, this won't do. Look for Jean-Marie Le Pen ...

"They like the movie Rabbi Jacob!" (Famous French movie starring Louis de Funès)

Voila a good reason, because we would love to dance like Rabbi Jacob and do as much good to the French as Louis de Funes did, but not there yet.

"They are secretly in love with Bar Rafaeli!"

Our French Old Charmers' souls which always have "in our shirts a letter to Clorise" (Cyrano de Bergerac) would indeed be charmed by "this perfect work that Heaven has shaped," but to a certain extent, as after that it becomes a psychiatric case....

"These are reactionaries who admire the IDF"

Not false! When we see the masterful spankings inflicted to dictators and other Arab bawlers of the area, yet largely superior in number and equipment and who left crying, we can stop smiling!

"These are Neo-Nazis who support a Nazi occupation!"

It is advisable to stop watching YouTube videos, learn to read and buy a history book before churning out so much crap by the meter.

"With this one, I got you" They are Islamophobic! "

Is there, at any point of this book, the least vicious and psychiatrically phobic attack, as insinuated by the use of the suffix "phobic" against Islam as a religion, against the Muslim faith as spirituality or against the Muslims as believers, or even against the Arabs as a race or ethnicity. We have the right not to adhere to the religious theses of Islam, we even have the right to reject the Islamic life model, and the right to have a critical opinion on the political implications of the Islamic religion and history without being treated as a hateful and paranoid neurotics. And rejecting Islam as a society model, as a political inspiration, and opposing its darker aspects does not prevent us from recognizing the history of Islam, of admiring some aspects of the Arab-Muslim civilization and even wishing for the preservation of its memory.

For instance, the Aztecs have shaped a brilliant, fascinating, complex civilization, which gave a lot to the culture of humanity. It is a civilization that must be studied and whose heritage and history must be preserved, including its religious and spiritual aspect. But would the first Aztec descendant, in France or elsewhere, start making human sacrifices and demand respect for the murderous aspects of his religion for the sake of his sensitivity, he will immediately be opposed to the principles which oppose the Radical Islam's misdeeds, and he could accuse everyone of Aztequophobia, he would not succeed.

What is the issue in the case of Israel is not Islam as such, the Muslims as such or the Arabs as such. What is at stake is the political side of Islam that a fringe of fundamentalist wants to apply and thus impose an Islamic sovereignty over all the lands claimed by Muslim conquests. It is the religious fanaticism within Islam that has led some to want to apply to the letter the genocidal Hadith texts and official biographies of Muhammad about the Jews. This is the Arab nationalism, may it be hidden under a religious aspect or carried by pan-Arabic national socialist theses.

In summary, it is the totalitarian aspects of Islamist or anti-Zionist theses based on Islam which are the issue and certainly not Islam in general and without distinction, in the wonderful amalgam of which are accused his opponents but which is made by its defenders .

"So why support Israel when one is not Jewish?"

This will be the conclusion shaped as a call to awareness.

We thought we won the Second World War but the Brown Plague is coming back. We thought we won the Cold War but the Red Plague is just getting smarter and devious. We were not suspicious, we thought we had vanquished. But we woke up in a world where freedom is dying, where the state of law is replaced by the welfare state, where technocracy trumps democracy with the complicity of the people fed-up of having to be clever.

The obscurantism, superstition, tyranny, feudalism, etc., everything against which we fought in 1642 in England, in 1776 in America, in 1789 in France and 1801 in Haiti come back with a vengeance, under new seductive, pragmatic or glimmering assets or under aspects of barbaric violence and fundamentalist religious indoctrination. Under the multiple assaults of those who want its death for political or religious reasons, we are in the twilight of the Free World which has already been largely conquered, and Israel is like the last legionnaires Camaron, like the last carre at Waterloo, the last bastion, the ultimate symbol of the defeat of freedom, justice, law and equality.

Israel is the last fortress that must be shot to recreate the world, redraw the maps, redefine the human up into his soul, r Israel is the last fortress that must be shot to recreate the world, redraw the maps, redefine the human up into his soul, reframe the relationship between humans. Israel, this old people whose national history is the Bible, represents the last anchor of a Western world based on a Judeo-Christian scheme of thought in constant renewal and that cannot be reduced to its past mistakes, to its sometimes heretics dogmas and its temporal interpretations of specific situations. Even the notions of love between men commonly called humanism, brotherhood, equality and even freedom, which may seem paradoxical to all those who see the Judeo-Christian model as a constraint, are rooted in the Jewish tradition, extended by Christianity which, alas, got often lost along the way just because it lost its Jewish roots.

The State of Israel, based on the obvious legitimacy of the Jews on this Mediterranean shore and based on this model democracy of free men, enlightened and equal, that its people had largely inspired and contributed to found, is the home of the Jewish people who represents the soul of humanity. It suffices to look at the long and historical list of its enemies, from the Roman Empire to the Catholic

Inquisition, and from Nazism to the Islamic State, which are also those of humanity, to be convinced.

So we must defend Israel as much as possible and to the end, by necessity of survival and assurance, for our children, of a free world based on human rights and the responsibility of equal and fraternal citizens.

And that is precisely the free men and women, non-Jew but aware of this war of attrition against everything we believe in, and that Israel wages by hook or by crook, for the last 67 years, to fight and prevent the Star of David flag from falling.

ABOUT THE AUTHOR

Who cares, it's not him that matters but his ideas

Translated from French by
MARLENE FERRON